THE DEVIL YOU DON'T KNOW

The Devil You Don't Know

A Play

Joel Thomas Hynes & Sherry White

Killick Press
an imprint of Creative Publishers

St. John's, Newfoundland and Labrador
2010

Canada Council for the Arts Conseil des Arts du Canada Canada Newfoundland Labrador

We gratefully acknowledge the financial support of the Canada Council for the Arts, the Government of Canada through the Book Publishing Industry Development Program (BPIDP), and the Government of Newfoundland and Labrador through the Department of Tourism, Culture and Recreation for our publishing program.

Cover Design by Todd Manning
Layout by Joanne Snook-Hann
Printed on acid-free paper

Published by
KILLICK PRESS
an imprint of CREATIVE BOOK PUBLISHING
a Transcontinental Inc. associated company
P.O. Box 8660, Stn. A
St. John's, Newfoundland and Labrador A1B 3T7

Printed in Canada by:
TRANSCONTINENTAL INC.

Library and Archives Canada Cataloguing in Publication

Hynes, Joel, 1976-
The devil you don't know / Joel Thomas Hynes & Sherry White.

A play, based on the novel Down to the dirt, by Joel Thomas Hynes.
ISBN 978-1-897174-56-2

I. White, Sherry, 1972- II. Hynes, Joel, 1976- . Down to the dirt.
III. Title.

PS8615.Y54D47 2010 C812'.6 C2010-901529-0

for Percy

Two of the most powerful voices in Atlantic Canada team up to breathe dramatic life into Hynes' internationally acclaimed prose. Based on the stunning novel Down to the Dirt, The Devil You Dont Know *is at its heart a love story of uncompromising brutality, honesty, and yes, beauty.*

– Robert Chafe, playwright, author of *Tempting Providence*

Funny, touching, and sometimes heartbreaking, but always achingly true to life. One of the best nights I've ever spent in the theatre.

– Mary Walsh

Intense, raw and visceral theatrical experience.

– CBC Radio

Hynes and White's dialogue has utilitarian, unpretentious snap!!

– Now Magazine

... a laugh riot!... thoroughly engaging and so true to life.

– The Telegram

HISTORY OF *THE DEVIL YOU DONT KNOW*

The Devil You Dont Know originally premiered through the Resource Centre for the Arts Theatre Company in St. John's, Newfoundland, at the LSPU Hall, has since been produced in Toronto at Theatre Passe Muraille, and an excerpt was published in the anthology *He Speaks! Monologues for Men*, available through Playwright's Canada Press. Originally starring Joel Thomas Hynes and Sherry White and directed by celebrated playwright/teacher/director Lois Brown, *The Devil You Dont Know* earned audience and critical acclaim, with CBC Radio Weekend Review dubbing it an "…intense, raw and visceral theatrical experience…."

INTRODUCTION

In 2003 I was asked to dramaturge and direct RCA Theatre Company's main-stage production of *The Devil You Dont Know*. Sherry and Joel were exciting young actors – emotional, outspoken, generous, intense and inspiring. Their play was a psychological unfolding of the experiences of two young lovers, told with humour and a visceral poetry in the Newfoundland dialect. This was exactly the kind of theatre of which I wanted to be a part.

In *The Devil You Dont Know* Keith Kavanagh and Natasha Healy attempt to escape their rocky home for the greener pastures of the mainland. A derelict Romeo follows his desperate Juliet to Halifax. This particular story of star-crossed lovers is full of drunken-longing, humiliating despair, willful mistakes. No double suicides for Keith and Natasha, instead a long howl of loneliness, as they tell that most common of Newfoundland stories – a search for a better day.

The play is structured like the opening of a wound, book-ended as it is by Keith's attempts to explain himself. The challenge of the bucket of stones he brings on stage during the opening monologue, for the use of those without sin, remains only until the end of the play. Time's up. Keith exits with his bucket in tact.

Adapted from Joel's manuscript for his book *Down to the Dirt,* Sherry White gave Natasha bite and howl to easily match Keith at his worst. Her monologue on the toilet as she drunkenly exchanges dignity for bravado is wrenchingly intimate.

The premiere of *The Devil You Dont Know* at the LSPU Hall marked a significant moment in time for Newfoundland theatre. The theatre voices of Joel Thomas Hynes and Sherry White are steeped in our accent, our dialect, and not just our experiences and our prejudices – our lies to ourselves, our truths and determination – our blackest of black humour; but our way of telling a story. CODCO, The Mummers Troupe and Sheilagh's Brush – the theatre voices of Newfoundland renaissance, as Sandra Gwyn so aptly named it (Saturday Night, 1976), had finally given birth to its child.

Following in the tradition of thirty years of Newfoundland theatre and Canadian collective creation, Joel Thomas Hynes and Sherry White created and performed the characters of Keith and Natasha, shaping them out of their own bodies and souls. With Joel and Sherry performing, playwriting and acting remained inextricably linked, but this play made no attempt to be legendary, to celebrate, or to be purposefully comic. The humour arose from the irony inherent in telling the story in the past tense. For thirty years, our theatre had proved, provided and invigorated our cultural psyche through our mostly collectively-created theatre. *The Devil You Dont Know* had nothing to prove. It stood on that tradition, drilled down beneath it, and told a story from the core of that psyche. The production was a revelation. Here was a new journey into the Newfoundland experience: a play with a singular and sophisticated Newfoundland voice telling a rich story broken off the Newfoundland soul.

The publication of *The Devil You Dont Know* is long overdue and hopefully this important and hard-cutting Canadian play will be celebrated with many new productions.

Lois Brown —
playwright / director / performance artist

Act 1 Scene 1

KEITH walks into the spotlight. He lays a huge bucket of rocks on the stage.

KEITH – That's exactly the point I was tryna make in the first place. Thank you kind sir. Or Madame. So hard to tell these days. The point is that we all have our fair share of devils. Hovering over the morning coffee. Now I'm hardly tryna pass myself off as the exception, dont get me wrong. But I would like to say, cause I'm sure as fuck no one's gonna say it for me, I would like to impart that despite it all I'm really not that bad. I'm not. I mean I owns a cat. Might not know where he's at all the time but I do own a cat, that's gotta say something for me. Ah, I dont smoke in bed so much anymore. *Since the Fire*, he says. What else? I dont throw stuff on the ground. I dont rob stuff…from people I knows. I'm not goin around slashin tires no more. I present meself to you tonight as a modern Catholic in saying that I'm really not that bad. So. When the time comes, and the time will come, when you're wishin you'd brought a Louie-ville slugger along to the show, or you're looking around for something you could possibly fashion a good noose out of, I'm gonna ask you to try, please just try, take a deep breath, and consider your own devils and how they sometimes deal with you.

He gestures towards the bucket of rocks.

In any event, I'll leave these here for y'all. And we can call this a 'cast the first stone' type of situation if you'll allow me the indulgence. And at some point, and G-d help us all if that time comes, when I feels the big crunch on the side of me skull and I'm headed face and eyes onto the floor, I'll try, in my final moment, when I'm gurgling my last breath, I will try and allow that who-so-ever cast that first stone has either risen above his (come to think of it now I have had women throw rocks at me before), has risen above his or *her* own devils to conclude that 'yes, that's exactly what that little fucker needs is a good chunk of rock in side of the face'. Or I'll assume that I've crossed some line. Which is not so hard to fathom, I s'pose. Either way, I forgive you in advance. Because that's the kind of fella I am. I'm really not that bad.

Keith walks off stage. Fade to black.

Scene 2

A clock ticks, slightly faster, more frantic than a normal clock. Lights come up slightly. The clock fades. It's late in the night. NATASHA cuts through the small living room and ducks into the bathroom. The sound of breaking glass. Moments later Keith creeps onstage with a baseball bat raised above his head.

K – Listen. Hear that? That was the blink of an eye. The sound of a heart tryin not to beat.

He raises the bat, steps closer to the bathroom door.

K – I never left that light on…

Closer

K – Alright! Well c'mon if you're comin. You picked the wrong fella to fuck with this night. I'll give ya to the count of three. One. TWO. Three!

The bathroom door swings open just as Keith would have made contact with it. Natasha walks out, a toothbrush sticking out of her mouth. Keith tries to hide the bat.

K – Jesus Christ Tash. Sorry girl.

Natasha – What were you gonna do Keith? Bash my head in?

K – I thought someone was breakin in –

N – Who'd break in here? It's a dump. A deathtrap.

K – I dont know. I'm half asleep girl –

N – So what, you charge at me with a bat?

She flops down on the couch. Keith eyes her from across the room.

K – Well it's nice to have you home, I must say.

N – Right.

Keith crouches over her and starts trying to undo the button of her pants.

K – Think we might try and have a bit of fun tonight? Been a while now.

She pushes him away.

K – Ahh, c'mon girl. Let's curl up and watch a skin-flick.

N – No Keith. I dont wanna watch a skin-flick or play with any poppers or cock-rings. I said no. Not yet.

K – Well when then? How long do you need?

N – I dont know. Not like my emotions are set to some kinda timer that tells me when it's alright to get down on all fours again.

K – Sure we dont have to do it that way.

N – I'm not having sex Keith. It's false.

K – What's that even mean? False?

N – Keith please, can we just go to bed out of it?

K – Now see, there's the idea…

N – Oh for fuck sakes.

K – I'm only jokin with you girl. C'mon then. I'm tired too.

Keith sulks off to the bedroom. Natasha starts after him, but stops and turns to address the audience.

N – Alright. I know I'm supposed to feel guilty. But I dont. Well, maybe I feel a little guilty for not feeling guilty.

Natasha walks off into the bedroom. Lights down.

Scene 3

Lights up. Morning. Natasha enters, surveys the room. She's wrapped in a sheet.

N – So close to escaping all this shit. Free ticket to Toronto. Decent job waiting for me. Apartment all lined up. I got on that plane, without Keith, and I wasnt lookin back. But it's like he found some way to hide in my suitcase and tag along just to spite me.

K (OS) – Tash? Natasha?

N – Out here.

Keith enters from the bedroom. Natasha, seated at the kitchen table rolling cigarettes. Keith has a good look at the audience.

K – Greener pastures in Toronto. Yeah. Yeah.

Natasha sits down on the couch. Keith takes her place at the table.

N – Everything good in my life is only good because it makes you feel bad. Therefore I am evil.

K – You cut me off. You cant just do that to someone.

N – The job in Toronto was just one more thing I had to rub in his face.

K – Cold as ice while I was bawlin, sobbin me guts out like some nancy-boy.

to Natasha

I mean, I can understand your being excited to go, but you could have felt *something* for me. Pretended to even.

N – Should see this place after one of his tears. Broken glass all over the place. Bits of furniture. Piss. Vomit. Macaroni.

to Keith

It dont even make sense for *me* to own anything. You'll only sell it or break it. Or Piss on it.

K – Laughed at me. Cause I was weak and you were gettin stronger.

to audience

That's the way it always is I s'pose: the one who walks away first carries all the power. And I didnt see it for the blessing it could have been.

N – Look, this trip to Toronto was the answer to everything. And I had to go shag it up by gettin pregnant.

K – When I got that phone call tellin me she was knocked up, my first reaction was complete and utter disbelief. Not shock, I just didnt believe her. It all sounded a bit too convenient for my liking.

N – Haul it out before you comes Keith. Haul it out *before* you comes.

K – The night before she left we had sex, like ya would, and it was pretty intense. Break up sex. And…well… towards the end I just couldnt pull out of her. Not right away.

N – I was only in Toronto a few weeks and they got hard as rocks.

cups her breasts

Rocks. I remembered my cousin, her first trimester, you couldnt go near her for the pain in her tits. All I could think was *jesus, jesus, je-sus*.

K – But I was good and able to let her go once she was gone to Toronto. That was the...irony. I wasnt the volatile, blubbering, desperate mess we both expected me to be. I was movin on. And suddenly she's tellin me we're gonna be bound to each other *by blood* for the rest of our lives. Pregnant, I said. Pregnant? Jesus.

N – Jesus. Jesus. Jesus.

K – I hoped to Christ she wasnt thinkin of havin it.

N – How could I even consider it?

K – Not this day and age. We're not exactly what you'd call career people. We dont even sit down and eat with one another.

N – And sure I'm after catchin Keith guzzling the mouthwash.

Keith laughs proudly. Gets up and paces across the room during the following. He's on the couch next to Natasha, mirroring her position. He takes his place on the couch beside Natasha.

K – Look here, relationships are preconceived by fate. It's all written down in some big ledger in the sky that says 'Okay, they'll meet here on this particular date, they can have this much of a go at each other, they will be granted sufficient notice before termination, and they will simply *end* on this particular date.

N – I prob'ly woulda miscarried anyhow. I'm not that healthy. I smokes like a tilt.

K – Myself and Tash had gotten all the warning signs, received our notice in the mail long ago, balled it up and tossed it in the stove.

Natasha gently lays her hands on Keith's.

N – I just cant imagine I'm even capable of having a baby.

Keith pulls his hand away dismissively.

K – So, even if I did entertain the notion of fatherhood, it was only for that one, brief, fleeting moment.

N – I'd like to though. Someday.

Keith jumps from the couch and lunges at the audience.

K – I slept with a girl named…ah…Monica, on the last night before the big day. Natasha up in Toronto, tossin and a-turnin. I s'pose I just didnt wanna be alone.

The phone rings. Keith saunters over to the table and picks it up.

K – Hell-o.

N – I'm lonely.

K – You'll be alright girl. How ya doin?

N – Scared, I guess. I wish you were here.

K – Me too. I wish you were here.

N – I love you.

K – Puss-cat is here. He misses you.

N – I said I love you.

K – I heard you. I love you too.

N – Can we be different this time Keith?

K – Yes. Yes we can.

Keith muffles the phone with his hand and nods toward the audience.

K – Things were gonna be different alright. That's prob'ly half the reason I got off with Monica. Bang another nail into the coffin. I forced Toronto and abortions and all the rest of that shit down into the back of my head. I knew what I done. She'll live with this now for the rest of her days. And all because I thought she was gettin the upper hand.

Natasha pulls a pair of women's underwear from beneath the cushions of the couch.

N – Keith? Who's that I hears in the background? Is there someone with you? Keith?

She huddles her knees to her chest. The lights close in on her. Keith gently hangs up the phone.

K – I guess right then and there I made up my mind to leave Natasha. I mean, I'd be there, verbally, say all the right things to help her through the aftermath. But I'd never *be* with her again.

The lights close in on Natasha. She appears very alone on the couch.

N – While I was up there shrinking and bawling, curled up with the fear and the guilt and heartache beyond anything *I'll* ever feel again.

K – Yeah, yeah, yeah.

N – I woulda given anything for even a familiar hand to hold, at the time.

K – Then she got talkin to a friend of a friend who said I was bein a “bad boy” in her absence.

N – While he was home here, balls deep in some slut from George Street.

K – And for some reason I denied it. She hung up. I called back. Musta left her a dozen messages, pretty much begging her to call me back, let me know she was alright. I mean, I’m not heartless.

N – Monnn-ICK-a

K – But I never heard a peep out of her till she showed up here on the doorstep a couple of weeks ago. All dramatic and wantin to work things out. So, you know, everything’s back to normal now.

Lights down.

Scene 4

Keith is no longer in the room. Natasha enters, loaded drunk. She opens her empty suitcases and starts packing.

N – Yes you're a good boy. And yes you're so smart and talented and yes the world owes you a favour. I have had it! Mommy and Daddy not loving enough. Teachers and cops too narrow minded, out to crush his free-spirited nature. I'm tired of just sticking it out, surviving. I wanna get ahead for a change, get out into the world and live. At least *feel* like I'm living.

Natasha keeps on packing, moves on to the next suitcase.

N – Thinks he's the big tortured poet. Well I'm creative. But I never have the room to move or think or friggin breathe, so how could I express it. I have been dreaming and planning this getaway and, ya know, the only thing that's been stopping me is the thought that if I dont look after him, he'll die. And no one else will ever love me. Christ. Well, die if you must Mr. Dark Depression, cause I'm movin to Halifax and I'm gonna be an actress.

Natasha pulls off her black wig and slams it into her suitcase. Turns out she's a natural blonde. She steps up on her suitcase, arms outspread.

N – That's right. I'm movin to Halifax and I'm gonna be an actress!

Keith walks in from the cold. She stands with her back to him. He sizes things up, doesnt speak.

N – I'm leaving Keith. I'm movin to Halifax.

K – What? For how long? Sure you're not home two weeks hardly.

N – My flight is booked for tomorrow morning.

K – Tomorrow morning Natasha? Jesus, nothing like a bit of notice. How long?

N – Maybe a few months…

K – Sure that's a goddamn lifetime. How long have you known?

N – Last week sometime, I guess.

Natasha goes into the bedroom.

K – You've known for a week that you're takin off and you picks the night before to let me know?

N (O.S.) – You knows what our week woulda been like Keith. It'd be Hell.

K – Well maybe we mighta found some better way to spend our time than watching foolish movies and talkin shit.

Natasha re-enters with a load of junk from the bedroom.

N – So I talks shit do I?

K – Well *I* tends to when I'm bored outta my bloody skull.

N – Well there you go. What do you need me around for anyhow, if you're so bored with me?

K – Tash, stop it. What are you gonna find in Halifax that you cant have right here?

N – I'm gonna look for some work in the theatre up there.

K – Theatre! Ha. Are you mental? Doin what?

N – Acting Keith. Maybe.

K – Buncha cut-throat fairies and lizzies dancin around a stage like…

N – Alright Keith.

K – Theatre…

N – Look, the very fact that I wants to be an actress and you never knew it, never even asked me about it, should tell you something. Should tell you that this might be a good thing. For me.

K – But how's it good for me? Alright for you when you falls down. Just pick up the phone and it's Daddy's wallet to the rescue…

N – I'm sorry I dont have the big black tragic relationship with my parents!

K – Dont try and turn this into a counseling session.

N – Well I dont need to feel guilty for having something you dont have.

K – You hardly got your foot in through the door and you're takin off again? It's startin to look like you're fixing to get clear of me.

N – Look around you Keith. It's a little dungeon. Expect me to spend the rest of my days cramped up here? Look.

She picks up a box of cat food from the table a shakes it.

N – Is this my cat?

She points to a Kerouac poster on the wall.

N – Am I the Jack Kerouac fanatic around here?

She points to a bulky looking shortwave radio.

N – Would I own that thing? This place isnt me. Only proof that I even live here is the phone bill and the lights and the lease…

K – "This place isnt me." Sure you got half the place stuffed into them bags.

N – Oh fuck off.

Natasha starts rolling a cigarette at the table.

K – I pays just as much or more here as you do. Where did that tobacco come from? Think I hauled that outta my hole or something?

N – Mine. All mine. If Natasha buys the tobacco then it's *everybody's*. If Keith buys it, it's *his*, but she can smoke away if she wants to. You horde like a youngster raised on second-hand toys.

K – What the hell is that supposed to mean?

N – It means I need some space Keith.

K – Space? You want fuckin space? Well here…

He grabs up Natasha's suitcases and heaves them out the door.

K – You wants goddamn space, you got it. Here…

He tears down the Kerouac poster and violently rips it to pieces.

K – Put up your fruity ornaments and pink-lemonade Breezeway bullshit. See if I cares.

N – You are making this so easy for me Keith.

K – When has it ever been hard for you Natasha?

N – Well it certainly wasnt very hard the other night. Not for long anyways.

A long pause between them. They stand and stare each other down.

K – Fuck you. I was drinkin all night long. That's when you picks your moment to want to be close. "Let's be close Keith. Let's be intimate" And I'm s'posed to find that kinda talk arousing? All bad enough with you just lyin there like a dead moose and me having to slave my guts out to get *you* off when all I wants to do is get off you…

N – Nice Keith. Well done. I had no idea I was so boring in bed. Why dont you run downtown and pick up one of your floozy sluts? Go find Monica.

K – Who's Monica?

N – Go give her your sob story about the horrible girlfriend you're chained to who's so boring in bed cause she wont let you shaft her in the ass.

K – Natasha…

N – That's all you wants isnt it? For me to just bend over and spread my asshole wide open? Nice and tight and you dont have to look at my face. Right? Well here…

Natasha drops her pants to her ankles and shoves her arse towards Keith.

N – C'mon then, give it to me you big stud. Let's pretend you found me down at the Sundance.

K – Pull your pants up Tash. There's enough of a stink in this room.

Natasha pulls her pants back up and hauls on her jacket. She gathers up her bags and heads for the door.

N – Oh that's right. You dont work so well under pressure do you? I forgot. Sorry.

Keith looks at the door for a long time, but doesnt follow her. Lights down.

Scene 5

Lights up. The apartment is a disaster zone. Keith is wearing pathetic long underwear and one sock. He's flaked out on the couch with the phone in his hand. The dial tone is louder than life. He slams the phone down.

K – How far out there do you have to put yourself before you gets a little humanity in return? Call me back. Keep in touch.

He staggers over to the TV stand and picks up a jagged old kitchen knife. He holds it up and walks into a red spotlight.

K – Let me know if you're still alive at least. Oh, but I'm strong. Keith Kavanagh? Tough as nails. I'm tough as…

He presses the blade against his forearm.

K – …fuckin…

He begins to move in reverse, like rewinding a video tape. Traces his steps back to the point where he slams the phone down, gets the busy signal, redials, till he's actually talking to Natasha.

K – Are we broke up or not?

Lights up on Natasha in her apartment in Halifax.

N – Keith, I have to write this thing…

K – Tell me!!!

N – It's my audition piece. I'm stressed out about it.

K – Well I have a life too. Now answer the goddamn question so I can go get on with it.

N – How am I stopping you from living your life Keith?

K – Well you're not there when I calls. You dont call when you says you're goin to. How am I s'pose to…function when you wont even give me a straight answer?

A car horn blows outside Natasha's apartment.

N – Look Keith, I have a lot of work to do.

K – Do you love me?

N – Of course I do.

K – And do you know…

N – Yes Keith I know how much you love me. I really have to go.

K – Are we finished? Is it over?

N – I'll talk to you later Keith.

K – But are we broke…

N – No! Alright? Happy? Now I'll talk to you later. Bye.

Lights down on Natasha. Keith retraces his steps in 'fast-forward' until he's again standing before the audience with the blade to his forearm. He pulls the knife across his flesh.

K – Tough as fuckin nails. Ahhh… shit.

Lights down.

Scene 6

Lights up. Keith is on the couch. He awakens with a jolt. It is dawn outside his window. A crow calls in the distance.

K – Ya know, I woulda been content to have died in a ditch playing G.I. Joe, and never known any other life. Way back when.

The phone starts ringing. He watches it ring until it stops.

K – A month now. Tonight will be my thirty-first night up pacing the floors. Imagine a fine handsome fella like myself up pacing the floors over some young one. I mean, I'm hardly stupid. I knows there's something goin on with her. I can feel it in my guts. I shouldnt have to beg to be number one on her list. I'm her goddamn boyfriend. But no, always rushin off to some bar or some new show with her new muppet-faced theatre-slop suck-hole friends. Any old excuse to excuse herself from what I'm sure must be the agonizing ordeal of talkin to me. Opening gala this and closing night that. Something's goin on. And if she cant muster up the guts to tell me over the phone, if she cant just let me go, let me move on and get on with it all…I'm just gonna have to track her down and see for myself. Yes by Christ. And if any of her little actor friends gets in my way I'll crack 'em in half. Yes I will. Fuck it what? *I'm* goin to Halifax.

Lights up on Natasha in Halifax.

N – What am I supposed to do when the right guy comes along? "No, sorry, I'd really like to fall in love with you but I've got this manic ex-boyfriend back home named Keith…" Well, to hell with that.

K – Shag it, I am goin to Halifax.

N – His name is Michel. Can you believe that? I met him in an acting class. He's really a director, but he said he likes to observe actors and their process.

K – I'm puttin my boots on!

N – He told me he really thinks I've got it. IT. So I said do you want some? Ha. No I never said that. But I did go out for a few drinks with him and before I knew it he was showing me the Alexandra Technique on his living room floor. And…anyway, we…well we've been having a pretty good time…He's got a great apartment. You can see the bridge. Lots of space, lots of nice furniture…

Keith covers his ears as though he can hear every word she's saying.

K – Ahhhh la la laaaaa, la la…

N – My first time…on a waterbed. And we talk too. Talk about everything and nothing. And, I dont know. You never know. He just might be the one.

K – Yes by Christ. Halifax it is.

Fade to black.

Scene 7

Lights up on Keith. He's dressed head to toe in black leather. He's out on the highway with his thumb out. A car passes by. He drops his arm.

K – You wanna know how I knew she was the One? I guess you could call it our 'first date'.

The sounds of a bonfire fill the air. Keith crouches into the light of the flames.

K – Big old bonfire into the Devil's Kitchen. She had a boyfriend but I didnt give a fuck. We'd been hangin out all evening, flirtin with each other. Foolin around.

Natasha joins Keith on stage. She's dressed in her original outfit, including her black wig. Keith whispers something in her ear and she smiles. He keeps whispering and she laughs unselfconsciously. She stops abruptly, suddenly nervous and uncomfortable.

K – Yeah, havin a fine time till Francey O'Dea reared his ugly head. What's wrong Natasha? What is it?

N – Nothing. I just think I'll go home.

Keith turns back to the audience.

K – Now I heard lots of rumours about Francey O'Dea messin around with young ones. Drivin down to the back of the graveyard in the nighttime. The ol' 'put out or get out' routine. Hard to know if any of it was true, but, Jesus, the look on Natasha's face, I knew something wasnt right.

N – Can we just go?

K – Look here, I'm not stupid. Now if you dont tell me what's goin on, I'm gonna go over there and boot him in the nuts. How's that?

Natasha laughs, despite herself.

N – Can we please drop it? He's not worth it. I'm fine.

Keith turns back to the audience.

K – Francey O'Dea, twirling his car keys like some fruit. He was at least six or seven years older than anyone at the fire. What business did he have? Sniffin around the young ones. Luring 'em into his cheesy car with that shoe-polish he calls hash.

Keith pulls a can of Pepsi out of his jacket and pops it open. He turns to Natasha.

K – I ever tell you about the time I fucked over this fella in La Manche Park with a can of this stuff?

N – What? You hit him with it?

K – No girl, Jesus no. He was a big fella. I poured it into his gas tank.

Natasha doesnt get it.

K – Sugar in the gas-lines. Engine ceases up solid. But real sugar is messy see, and you knows you're gonna get it everywhere.

Keith takes a sip of Pepsi.

K – But no mess at all with a Pepsi. And it does just as much damage as a whole bag of sugar.

Natasha laughs again and then stops herself, realizing something.

N – Francey O'Dea's sick, beastly eyes grazing over me from across the bonfire. And like always the choking, drowning, suffocating feeling in my lungs. The taste of bile in back of my throat. That quivering weakness in my knees making it impossible to even just walk away.

Natasha looks down and wollops her legs.

N – Walk away!! But I'm frozen to the spot and if he just wanted to walk over here and…

Keith holds the can of Pepsi out to Natasha.

K – You want the rest of that? Imagine we used to have this stuff in our baby bottles. And they wonders why we're all half cracked.

N – Francey drove a cheesy, souped up Monte Carlo with tinted windows. It was his baby. Fuzzy dice, eightball on the gearshift. The inside lined with those fuckin dingle balls. I heard some guys in school raving about how much horsepower it had. Well I didnt care then and there how many little horses I'd have to kill off. Fracey O'Dea had it coming for a long time.

Natasha turns to Keith.

N – You got a pocket knife?

K – What for?

N – Well I need something to open the airway dont I?

Keith hands her his knife. She starts to walk away, stops and turns back.

N – What if he catches me?

K – He wont.

Natasha walks into the shadows. Keith moves in close to the campfire.

K – B'ys who got a can of hairspray or something? I knows a little trick with the fire.

Natasha in the background crouches down next to Francey's car with the Pepsi.

N – I knew right then and there that me and Keith were in it for the long haul. Keith and Natasha, Natasha and Keith. Now say ahhhh…

Keith acting the fool around the fire to distract people.

K – I'm not fuckin jokin! I can knock out a cow with my bare hands. There's a little spot behind the ear see…

N – My jesus what was I doing? I'd be arrested. I'd be shot. I'd… Francey O'Dea had a good long walk ahead of him tonight. Time stood still. Nothing but the sound of Pepsi drizzling down into Francey O'Dea's gas tank. All the pain emptying out of me, floating up into the night. And the lighter the can got, the lighter I became.

K – And I knew, right then and there that she was the one. She is the one.

Keith and Natasha kiss. The lights go down to the sounds of Francey's car starting and stalling, stalling…

Scene 8

Present Day. Natasha, alone on stage. This is her audition piece in which she performs BOTH characters, going back and forth between the two. The first character is HOSTAGE WOMAN and the second is INTERROGATER, who speaks in a very bad, stereotypical French/German accent. Scene begins with Hostage Woman lying on the floor, beaten, exhausted, tortured…

HOSTAGE WOMAN

Please, have mercy. I'm ready...to talk. I will tell you everything you need to know. But first, please. I beg of you, a drink of water...my throat is so dry.

She reaches for an imaginary cup of water and chugs it back.

Ahhh...thank you. Now then, lets get it over with.

INTERROGATOR

Who assisted you in your escape? And please, no lies. You are not strong enough to have made it out alone.

HOSTAGE WOMAN

Look, it was me, all me, I swear. I'm stronger than you think…

INTERROGATOR

Hmmm...and where is your husband? It is ludicrous for a woman to travel alone in these dangerous times.

Interrogator kicks Hostage Woman viciously.

Surely there is a man?

HOSTAGE WOMAN
reacting to the blows

Surely there is not. There was once, long ago. But he slowed me down. I stole away at night while he slept and dreamed of me. I do not know what became of him.

INTERROGATOR
Hmmm...rest assured, it is not I who imprisons you, but your own refusal to co-operate. But we have our ways of extracting truth from stubborn women. Do you know what this is?

Interrogator discloses an imaginary instrument of torture. Hostage Woman recoils in alarm, screams and flies into a panic.

HOSTAGE WOMAN
No please!! I've told you all I know. Please...

Natasha's performance is suddenly cut short as the house lights come up.

N – What? But there's more. I wrote it myself...Oh really? Oh. I didnt realize...

She takes out a dictionary and flips through it.

But I thought a monologue, by definition, was, is, a dramatic or comic piece spoken entirely by one person? But it was *just me* speaking...oh, oh I see what you mean. Right. That makes sense. But, so, what if the character had multiple personalities or something...well she might have, you dont fuckin know...I'm not arguing with you...I just figured if I did both sides you'd see how versatile I was...well I was nervous...no I got experience...I was just *experimenting*...alright...So I'll pick something else for my call back?

Natasha sheepishly walks away.

Scene 9

Keith is out there on the highway, idle and hitching. He pulls a small notebook and pencil from his pocket. He starts to sing, rewriting certain lines and reworking the melody as he goes along.

K – Like a fresh and showered lover, naked, waiting on the other, she tasted just like summer in the coldest winter wind. But like a damp and broken cigarette in a nervous situation, she pulled him from her pocket and he let her down again.

Keith puts the notebook in his pocket. Straightens out for a passing car.

K – You know, you have to be very particular about what you carry in your pockets these days...that's how they'll judge you in the end. They'll find you scattered in bits, strewn across the highway with your head crushed and mangled and of course they'll search your pockets. So if you happen to be carrying the latest Stephen King novel, then that will be the level you achieved in reading. That will be the degree to which your literary tastes will have matured. And if you happen to have a big Nike swoosh plastered across your chest, they'll assume you spent your final moments in a feeble attempt to promote the corporate economic benefits of overseas slave labour to the fat bastard who knocked you down. Listen, you gotta keep yourself dressed for the weather this day and age.

Another car passes Keith by.

K – I'm mean, we'll all get a bit of a funeral out of it I suppose. The clock ticks ever closer towards that grand 3000.00 mahogany overcoat. There'll be all kinds of sentimental horn-tootin' going on. For a little while. Who you were, where you been. If you were rich you led a full life. If you were poor you led a good life. Then the world will move on. You'll be all but forgotten until one day your name'll pop up in association with some nasty misdeed and the fella says, "I remembers him. Sure he loved his hockey didnt he? Spent his final moments bleeding into a Habs jersey." And his buddy says, "No, no, no. You got it all wrong. He loved his beer. His shirt said Molson, not Montreal. It said 'I Am Canadian'." And your man in the corner pipes up and says, "I remembers him now. And here all this time I thought he was a Newfoundlander. Where the fuck was he from then? Who the fuck are we talking about? Well it's not my goddamn round, I bought the last two!"

Lights down.

Scene 10

Natasha's back in her apartment, cordless phone in her hand.

N – Hi. It's me. I waited for you after my audition, did you forget? Give me a call, bye.

Hangs up phone.

How come Michel didnt tell me about the monologue thing? He knew what I'd written, even gave me a few pointers about my German accent.

Picks up phone, dials again.

Hi Michel, I'd love to talk to you about my audition. The director was a fuckwad. Call me as soon as you gets in? Bye.

Hangs up phone.

Either he doesnt know as much as he says he does, or he *wanted* me to make a fool of myself.

Dials number again.

Hi, you can ignore that last message. I'm just wondering what kind of game you're playing here, because if you think you can just walk all over me you can think again Mr. Director.

Hangs up phone.

Me thinks he doesnt know who he is dealing with. My dear, there's nothing I wont do when I gets riled.

Dials number again.

And just so you know, you had a snot in your nose at dinner the other night, the whole time. But I let it go because I am an accepting and forgiving person. So if you call me back I might forgive you, bye.

Lights out.

Scene 11

P.A. ANNOUNCEMENT:
Ladies and gentlemen pleased be advised, the *S.S. Drowning Moose* will be docking shortly in lovely…downtown…North…Sydney. Where I met my wife…and settled down…all those years ago…yep, I'm a happy man, happy, happy, happy…

Keith is standing on the highway reading a book with a flashlight.

K – One of these days when I'm old and grey I'm gonna walk into that monstrous bookshop up on Kenmount Road with a big bag of books. I'm gonna dump them all out on the floor and say..."I stole every one of these books while...that fella right there was working." Ever rob a book? Easiest thing in the world. Just make sure you wear a good jacket. Hold the book in your hand and then, all in one move, this is the key, all in one move, crouch down to a lower shelf and slide the book up under your armpit. Grab another book of around the same size and colour on your way back up. The clerk would have to be pretty keen or pretty goddamn bored with their job to catch on to that one. Then you just browse for a bit as natural as possible. You'd be surprised at the size of the books you can get away with too. Go on then and ask 'em to locate a book that you know they dont carry, or one that doesnt even exist. "You got anything in by that Kavanagh fella...Keith Kavanagh?" This makes them feel as though they've let you down. All is left to do is to walk off looking disappointed. Easiest thing in the world.

Lights down on Keith and up on Natasha. She's got a huge plate of french fries and gravy in her lap.

N – I decided to cook up a few home fries while I was waiting. But as I was peeling the potatoes, I kind of trailed off, and peeled the whole bag - just a five pound bag. Anyway, I decided to cook them all and save some for later. And I had a few cans of mushroom gravy too, that mom sent up in a care package. I was gonna only cook *one* can, but then there were so many home fries, I thought, oh, I'd hate to run out of gravy before I run out of home fries. So I cooked all 3. Some delicious.

Lights down on Natasha and back up on Keith.

K – Oh dont get me wrong, I'm not a thief. I just think that there's different levels of thievery. Like that time I got picked up in to *Walmart* of all places. Oh I swiped a copy of Pink Floyd's 'the Wall'. Soon as I'm out through the door this big beefy jerk spins me around and tells me I'm under arrest for theft. Like Roger Waters would give a fuck. So I ends up in court and it's all a big joke to everyone. The judge says "So you're a big Pink Floyd fan Mr. Kavanagh?" And all these suit and tie guys are snickering and I says "I dont know b'y. I never got to watch the goddamn movie first nor last." I guess I should have gotten a lawyer for that one. But that's not stealing. From a multi-go-zillion dollar corporation like Walmart? Stealing is when your buddy gives you twenty bucks for a gram of hash and you pinches off a nickel for yourself. That's pure thievery. Not movies or books or...liquor for that matter. So yeah, I waltzed on in to the gift shop on the ferry and robbed a bottle.

He holds up a bottle of whiskey.

So what? You wouldnt know now but the liquor corporation were gonna go under or something. What are they selling liquor in a gift shop for anyhow?

He takes a slug.

They'll never miss it. But I certainly would. Out here on the road. Oh yeah. I swiped a bunch of Nevada tickets too. That's different though. What?

Back to Natasha. She is almost passed out in her chair. Her pants are undone. She's stuffed with french fries.

N – Ohhhh. Did the phone ring?

She picks it up, checks it.

I should have only opened the one can of gravy because, cause the first plate was soooo good. And then there was all this gravy left in the pot...so I had another plate. Big mound of them. And I decided to add ketchup too, for variety. Too much gravy though, cause I ate the fries, but then I was left with a plate full of gravy and ketchup. But it was so good, right? And I was that close...I would have had to throw it all away then, so I said fuck it, it's just one more plate, who's it gonna hurt? But it hurts. Ohhhhh it hurts bad.

Scene 12

Keith is still on the road. Another car passes by.

K – You know, I came a thousand clicks across the Island yesterday in under ten hours. Five, six rides at the most. Now I'm what? Where am I? Nova fuckin' Scotia. People looking at me like I'm some kind of Nazi.

Another car passes and Keith yells an obscenity at it. He mutters and paces for a bit. Another car passes and he drops to his knees.

K – God please just get me where I wants to go. I can turn things around for the better this time if you just give me one more ride. To the bus station in Truro even, I'll go from there...

Another car passes. Lights down on Keith and back to Natasha.

N – Okay, he didnt show up, but...just because Michel and I arent glued at the hip doesnt mean we're not serious. I'm an adult now, and I cant be involved in obsessive relationships. There's more at stake, I have a career to pursue. Michel is a grown man, with adult friends, some of whom are female, and that is totally cool.

She picks up the phone and dials again, then hangs up, annoyed. Lights down on Natasha and back on Keith. He is still on his knees.

K – I would sell my soul to the Devil you know. I mean I wouldnt do it now for a run to Halifax...but...you know and you'll say that to people and they think you're cracked. Like it's gonna happen.

He jumps to his feet and raises his arms skyward.

Well I says sign me up. Show me the crossroads or the black bogs or wherever it's supposed to go down and I'll do it. I will sell my soul to the Devil this very instant if he wants it.

Long pause.

See. There is nothing. Except the fact that we're all going down in that deep black hole in the ground. Eventually. That's all any of us knows for sure.

Keith straightens out for another car. It stops. He hesitates, and then runs toward it.

K – Right on. Thank you Jesus. *Lights down*

Scene 13

Natasha is stuffing a banana into her mouth as she speaks.

N – It's too bad, see, where I dont know Michel very well, I have ABSOLUTELY no idea what the password to his voicemail could be. He should have told me, cuz he could be dead or something, and the cops didnt know who to call, he lives alone you know. And I'd love to erase some of those messages. At least the snot one. And the bald-headed-quiff one, you didnt hear that.

Scene 14

Keith is on the road again. A car slows down, music blasting. The people inside laugh and shout at Keith. Someone throws a banana peel out the window and Keith picks it up.

K – Fuckin' Cape Breton Hippies. Draws animals out to the road. Didnt think about that did you? People says 'Oh but it's just a banana peel, it's biodegradable'. Well if you've ever had to finish off a twenty-pound beaver with a hockey stick you'd think twice about where you throw your peels. See, told you I'm not that bad.

Lights down on Keith and back on Natasha.

N – I got about *this* much patience. When, oh lord please tell me when will I learn? He *finally* answered.

Natasha speaks into the phone.

Belinda, is she your sister? Your Stage Manager? Ohhh...are you directing a show now? Can I be in it?

To audience.

I dont buy it for a minute. Anyway, I apologized profusely for the messages, told him I was suicidal about the audition, and hinted around long enough till he finally invited me on this dinner date.

Speaks into the phone again.

You sure I wont be imposing? Well, it will be great, I'm starving.

Hangs up.

Belinda. Sounds fat to me.

Natasha does up her pants and goes.

Scene 15

Keith pushes a bus seat onto the stage.

K – Fine. So I took the goddamn bus. Does that mean I failed? No. Just means I'm ahead of schedule.

He settles into his seat and gestures towards the phantom young woman at his side. He's loaded drunk.

K – Smell her? Fresh like that? That's that Sunflower for women. I robbed a bottle at a party in the Goulds one night for Natasha. She never wore it though.

Keith fidgets in his seat, goes to speak to the girl and remembers himself.

K – She looks some good what? No matter what I wears or if I shaves and washes and combs I still feels like a dirt-bag. I dont know why. Money I suppose, that's what it all comes down to. They can smell the empty pockets a mile away.

To himself.

Hi. Ahem. Hi. My name's Keith. Hello. Good evening. I'm Keith. I'm Keith Kavanagh. I'm Keith-goddamn'-Kavanagh. You knows who I am...I'm Keith-fuckin-Kavanagh. Hi. Howdy.

She supposedly asks him his name.

My name? Ahhh, Jacob. Melissa. Melissa. Oh, I dont know about that. I woulda swore your name was Charlene. I dont know you just looks like a Charlene. You know how some people have that look like they should have been named something else? Actually, come to think of it now I went out with a girl named Melissa one time and her most profound realization was that her black lipstick made her teeth look too white. So why dont we go with Charlene for now? Ah, I'm coddin' around. Wanna drink?

He pulls out the bottle.

Whiskey says I. Mix? Dont be so foolish girl. The mix is what kills you. I wouldnt drink it any other way. Sacrilege. Go on look. No harm in it. Me? Well, I'm on my way into town to meet my cousin Keith. He's half cracked. He's one of those guys you know, bit of a genius, walking the fine line? Gonna spend the weekend on a big tear. Gawd help us all. Well, right now I'm working on a book of prose poetry. Really. What do you mean I dont look like a poet? Fuck does a poet look like? What's it about? It's fuckin' poetry, it's not about anything. Here, have another swig of this. Have another little snort girl, wont kill ya. I'm not dead am I?

Keith freezes. Natasha walks into the scene as if time is standing still.

N – Sure Keith would screw anything. He would. I knows for a fact he's had sex with Ivana. Ivana was Tommy Bernard's "date" for a dance one night back in High School. They came, Ivana wearing a slinky red dress, Betty Boop hair, captivating blue eyes. Tommy was waltzing with her on the dance floor, squeezing her ass, hand up her skirt, all his cronies standing around snickering, thinking he was the king. Then him and his loser friends were in the cafeteria, they had Ivana under the table. They kept passing her back and forth putting her mouth on their crotches, pretending to orgasm. All the girls were standing around, giggling, wishing THEY were Ivana in the red dress. After, Tommy and them took her out on the dance floor again. Taking turns. Slow dancing, then, body surfing. Ivana would float up among the balloons and streamers, fall, land on her head. Then somebody else would go over and drop kick her into the air. Her arms and legs flapping, her red dress falling down around her shoulders, Betty Boop hair unmussed, eyes wide open. She had my ass. My lips. My cunt. First comes the flattery, the dancing, then the kissing and fucking, and then she gets tossed around like a soccer ball. She had 3 inviting loveholes, and *she* didnt put up a fight. I went over and took her, gave her my sweater. Me and Ivana walked into the bathroom, where I deflated her. Then I neatly folded her up and took her home. Anyways Keith found her in my closet last winter. I told him the story, but he didnt quite get it, surprise surprise. Now Ivana is missing in action, and *you know who* is my number one suspect.

Natasha walks away. Keith resumes his "talk" with the girl.

K – Well your fancy boyfriend means fuck all to me. What? Nothing. Talking to myself girl. Talking to myself. That's where you'll find the brightest conversation. Actually, I'll tell you a secret. I robbed this very bottle. I did. In the gift shop on the ferry. I just waltzed on in and took it. I dont give a fuck if someone saw me. No girl that's not true. I had this in the fridge this past two months now. I hardly ever drinks.

Pause. Keith looks towards the girl.

K – You have nice lips. Nice and full. You can lie down if you wants to. Make yourself comfortable. Go on look. Lie your head across my lap if you like.

Keith starts to undo his belt buckle and then suddenly scrunches aside to let the girl out of her seat.

K – What? I didnt mean it like that. You looked tired girl. Tired. Come on girl. I'm only joking around.

Keith takes another little swig and chokes on it. He lies down across both seats.

K – Jesus I thought she'd never leave me alone.

Natasha comes back into the scene. Keith is asleep on his back. She stands behind the seat looking down at him.

N – Blow job blow job blow job. There's girls I'm sure that Keith never even had a conversation with, but they've given him a blow job. And worse than that, is he loves jokin about blow jobs. I could kill. He'll gently run his hand through my hair, and stroke the back of my neck, and just when I starts to allow myself to be vulnerable, when I thinks he's genuinely expressin *warmth* towards me, he pushes my head down towards his crotch. And he thinks it's hilarious. It's too bad, cuz it really takes all the joy out of it. I use to think it was a nice place to go, where you'd just disappear into this, this place, where nobody'd interrupt you, or, or, try to connect or get you to open up. You're already there, connected, open, just rhythmically sucking. Your breathing regulates and you're whole body becomes engaged, and you just go with it. Up and down, in and out, drool flyin everywhere, all the better for lubrication. And the best thing is, your usually helping him, whoever the dick owner is, you're helping him disappear.

She spreads Keith's legs and unbuttons his pants.

N – Anyway, it's important that one of your hands is on the base of his wiener, while the other hand should be paying a bit of attention to his beans.

She gets down on her knees.

But I usually need one hand to hold myself up, to give me leverage. And I mean really, who's gonna complain?

You got their cock in your mouth. It dont get much better than that.

Natasha goes down on Keith. Lights out.

Act 2 Scene 1

Keith is sitting on a park bench in Halifax. Sounds of a busy city surround him.

KEITH – Well I suppose I'll let you in on a little secret. Alright? I aint never set foot outside of Newfoundland before. But what's to be afraid of? Really? Besides, I got a pretty good defense against the *booming metropolis* of Halifax and that's the common knowledge that they got no culture. Oh yeah, they got their little *lobster fishery* and they plays the bagpipes but they got no real culture. Sure the Scottish robbed the bagpipes from the Irish anyhow. Everyone knows that. Meaning that Nova Scotia is in possession of goods indirectly stolen from the better part of Newfoundland. That's the Southern Shore, the Irish fuckin' Loop in case you're wondering.

Keith starts to sing some drunken anthem which soon turns to howling. A police siren sounds, lights flashing. Keith gathers his bag and scrambles off into the night. Lights up on Natasha sitting in a bathroom stall.

NATASHA – So it turns out Belinda is a stripper. Michel happened to wander into a strip club one Tuesday at lunch time. He ordered bbq chicken wings, hot, and plunked himself down in front of the stage to have a feast. Out comes Belinda, swayin' to and fro, grinding up and down on the pole. And he's lickin' his fingers as she's dancing up a storm to Careless Whisper. He marvels at how good she can dance wearing nothing but heals. High high heals. And just as he is marveling at that fact, one heal breaks. As she's going down, she thinks to herself, "this is why they call them "factory seconds"," and she tumbles over and lands on Michel's plate of wings, knocking them on the floor. He saves her from a deadly fall to the ground, she saves him from an afternoon of heartburn and gas. Friends for life. This would be interesting conversation. Sure, I'd be jealous, maybe intimidated, but at least I wouldnt be bored out of my fucking skull!

Keith climbs up over a wire fence and jumps to the floor. He hurts his foot and limps into his light.

K – Never fails. In town ten minutes and I'm already a wanted man. For what? Singing? Jesus. I think it's broke. Shoulda seen me. I scaled that fence back there like it was a friggin' ahhh...well I suppose it was twenty feet.

N – And I just have to say, nobody offered me a part in this play they're talking about.

K – Shoulda seen the dirt that I saw through this basement window back there. This couple doing the business on an old couch. I stopped for a bit to have a gander. Buddy was on top and he was givin' it to her but she was just lying there, not making much of a fuss about it. He was a real metal head with his big hair flying all over the place and he still had his sneaker-boots and jeans on so I guess they were having a fast one. What? I was just passing a bit of time. The fucking cops were after me.

N – All lighting cues this, and set changes that. I thought theatre was about having a profound effect on people. I'd rather be a fucking collection agent.

K – But then all of a sudden missus pointed at me and Metal Head hauls his pants up and starts for the door. So I took off back through the yard and over the fence into the next yard. Five or six more times, up and over fences, lawn chairs and picnic tables, swing sets. I tripped in a fuckin' weed-whacker and I flattened on the concrete walkway.

N – She couldnt stage manage my hole. Oh, but she does know the difference between baklava and a bellaclava. Just shut up and let me order, terd! And what's with all the big words? WHO cares. I'm sorry I just dont "comprehend".

K – Gave my knee a good bang too. Dogs barking and lights were coming on in the yards behind me. I just kept running. I dont know where the fuck I am now. Dont know how I busted up my ankle either.

Lights down on Keith.

Scene 2

N – So I rolled my eyes a few times and snorted at a few jokes. He has the gall to ask to have a word with me in private, and then says to me, GROW UP? How am I supposed to grow up ON DEMAND? Can anyone tell me? Now I'm supposed to go back out there and sit across from her smug little, highly offended face, and spend the rest of a wasted evening being POLITE because I was told to. What a joke. I'm not going. I'll sit here until I rot before I go back out there and look like a fool.

Keith is flaked out in the middle of the road. The sounds of a crazy city all around him.

K – God, I'm so full of shit. Natasha's gonna welcome me though. You watch. She probably already knows I'm in town or at least on my way. We always had that kind of connection.

Keith sends a message into the night.

Alright girl. Here I am, come and find me. I'm all yours.

He waits a while and then stands up, favouring his foot.

She could be in some stud's bed with her wrists tied to the bedposts having a fine time for herself. NATASHA! Natasha! Naataashaa!

A police siren flashes again and Keith takes off.

Natasha swigs back her glass of wine. Looks at her glass longingly.

N – Frig this. Why should I be hiding away in the bathroom. I'm the one having sex with the guy, arent I? Not her. I should just go out there and eat till I puke, I'm not paying.

She goes out.

Scene 3

Keith is sitting on the bench again. Looking at the audience as if he were waiting for them.

K – Ah you missed it. You missed it. I was coming through the park there and I was ahhh...propositioned. Honest to God I thought I was gettin' mugged at first but...What have we here I said? Faded denim skirt, black tights, red cowboy boots with white trim, a black low cut blouse and a white leather jacket with fringes. There must be a Sally Anne around here somewhere. And she was standing right in front of my face, pushin' fifty if she was two days old.

Natasha comes stumbling onto the stage. She looks back over her shoulder and throws her purse down.

N – LIKE I WANTED TO EAT IN YOUR STUPID RESTAURANTE ANYWAYS. Morons.

She goes back for her purse and sits on the side of the building.

I could use the walk home, I need to work off that big piece of balaclava I ate for desert. I go to this supper, and the minute I get the hint that he might be interested in the other woman, I'm just supposed to politely excuse myself and walk home with my tail between my legs? It's not that complicated, he could have told me before dinner, "Natasha, I'm interested in somebody else." "Natasha, you're too good for me." They kept exchanging these quick little knowing glances. Then Belinda asks me how old I was, and I said "22, I'll be 23 on my birthday" which is obvious I know, but what I meant was, I'm actually closer to 23 than to 22, but Belinda puts her head down, trying to hide that she was laughing at me. I waited until she looked up again, and when she did, I threw my drink in her face. Bitch. Then Michel rushes over to *her*. Like...what? What happened to Mister Love Nuts, who was all turned on by the faint smell of perspiration he got off of me the other morning, and wanted to bury his head in my armpit? Well you know what MICHEL? Take your soft spoken fruity voice, your Feldenkreis warm ups and morning roll downs, and take your short little stubby penis and shove it. ELSEWHERE.

She marches off.

K – I said "What do you mean this is where you work? What are you the park warden? Well how much do it cost?" I said, "for a good time like." "Twenty-five dollars," she says to me. "Twenty-five dollars? Do I look like I'm that hard up?" So I handed her a twenty and I said "that's all I got girl. Take it or leave it." And she took it. She wasnt getting one over on Keith Kavanagh by Christ. I'm slicker than that.

Keith takes a slug from the bottle.

She took me over behind some shack at the other side of the park. Her knee cracked as she eased herself down to the ground in front of me. She slid her hands up under my coat and I realized she was searching me, that even though her job must be jam-packed with glamour and perks, it wasnt without its share of risks.

Keith raises his arms over his head.

–I'm clean girl. Search away. I wouldnt harm a fly.
So she started in on me and I couldnt help wondering where that mouth was after being. I let my head fall back against the shack and waited for something to happen. Like ya would. And I dont know, I was all rearing to go on the way over. But something was definitely wrong. She was going up and down, up and down, squeezing and spluttering, but I wasnt responding at all.

Pause. Keith shakes his head, exasperated.

Finally I said "Ah shag it girl. Shag it. It's no use. I've been drinking since last Wednesday." I dont know. I never had it happen before. Well once or twice I suppose. But only when I'm drinking. Then she was gone, Sally Anne. She just took my last twenty bucks for not even ten minutes work. That's over a hundred bucks an hour for Christ's sake. And she wouldnt even hang around for a drink. I suppose I shouldnt even be at it considering the circumstances. Jesus, if Natasha ever found this out there'd be war. And sure she found out about Monica. I suppose I could've done without that little romp too. Anyhow you missed it...I guess this is as good a time as any to throw rocks at me now if you feel so inclined.

N – How come I can never keep a *nice guy*. I've done it all right, I've said my novenas. Well mom says 'em for me, but on my request. And all I get is the perverts and the rejects, and the nutcases. And Keith. Never the guys who do yoga, or clean house, or quit smoking. Not those guys, those guys think I'm scum. They think I'm TRASH.

She takes a flask and a wine glass out of her coat.

N – Well I'm not, cocksuckers. I AM NOT!

Swigs back the drink.

Keith has reached Natasha's house. He's standing outside sizing the place up.

K – So. This is it hey. Fuck. Where's the swimming pool. Where are all the bronze water sprites Ms. Natasha? The good life is it? Sure this place is no better than the apartment back home.

It obviously is.

Fuck it.

Keith starts pounding on the door.

Natasha! Natasha!

He finally gives up and sits down on her step.

It's two o'clock in the morning and where the hell is she? What am I, some kind of Leper having to roam around for a place to sleep?

Keith finally slumps down on Natasha's step.

N – Who wants a nice guy anyways? Nobody, that's who. Cause they are sickening. At least with Keith, if he's bawling it's because he sliced himself open with a knife. He's not afraid of pain. He's a real man. No he's not. And you know what REALLY makes me sick about me? When I was having sex with Keith, and I was looking at him and saying, "Haul it out before you comes," In my mind I was thinking, "Come inside me Keith, come inside me" Until I came. Then I run off, la de da, have an abortion, because it's my right, because it was a mistake, it was an accident. YES, it was a mistake, but I'm not stupid, I was screwing without a rubber, it was NO accident. But if I had that baby, it'd belong to social services right now.

Lights up on Keith on Natasha's step. He's lighting matches and tossing them on the ground.

K – It was like...like lighting matches and tossing them in the grass. And you watch it catch fire and your heart speeds up and you know you're supposed to stamp it now but you're hooked on this rush, this pumping, rip-roaring energy coursing through your veins...Next thing you know you're gonna be a Dad. Then the next thing you know your not...

N – There was a time between me and Keith that if one had the flu, the other wanted it. Anything that's in you, I want. I could kiss him deep first thing in the morning, his breath sour and shitty and me not caring, knowing I tasted the same or worse.

The sounds of cats fighting / fucking fills the night. Keith jumps with the fright.

K – Even them cats got a place to go lie down when they're done I bet. See the one doing the pushing, the tomcat I assume, with his two white paws in the back? Puts me in mind of Metal Head screwing missus with his sneaker-boots on. Even headbangers and tomcats got someone to love. There's people around, all over the world, curled up with their lovers in beds and on couches and poor Keith got no one cause he's too fucked up to hang on to anyone.

N – Why is love only pure and good in the beginning? Is knowing me such a complete friggin' turn off? Like his stupid ugly cowboy boots, he just *had* to have, they would make his life complete, a real rock'n'roller, and the first time he tried to wear them in a bit of snow, he was slippin all over the place, looking like an asshole, that's it then, fuck those cowboy boots. Sittin there in his room now, these 2 years. I AM THOSE COWBOY BOOTS! I AM THE SLIPPERY SOLES, tossed in the back of his closet. So I toot-scoot-n-boogied it out of there.

The sound of cats again.

K – Now. See the way they finished up. Just a howl and a shudder and then off in separate directions. Just the way love should be. No bullshit.

The wind picks up a bit, carrying the sounds of the city with it. Keith tries to warm himself.

K – They'll find me dead here. And Natasha'll curse herself and her cold notions for the rest of her days. I might even make the papers: "Newfoundlander Abroad Dies in Search of Love."

Keith jumps up and pounds on the door again.
He turns and yells at a passerby.

K – Have I got something on belong to you buddy? Well what the fuck are ya lookin' at? Yeah, keeping going is right. *Keith slumps back onto the step. Lights down.*

Lights up. Both Keith and Natasha begin to crawl / stagger simultaneously towards the audience, speaking at the same time.

N – Procrastination.

K – The fact of the matter is that life is long.

N – Like TV. That's all men are. "Yeah, maybe I'll get at that now, but first I think I'll watch one more show."

K – It's a long, drawn out, relentlessly disgusting ordeal. And all the while the heart keeps beating. And who for? People drifting in and out of our lives like smoke.

Dialogue overlaps.

N – And before you know it, years have passed you by, and you've done nothing but watch boring sitcoms and your ass has permanently gone to sleep. And you could have been *doing something*. Well that's IT. No more shows, no more distractions, no more guys. Life is just too short for all this shagging around.

K – So you know I will eventually get through with all this nonsense. And when I do I'll be making a few changes. I'll find me a place where people'll feel like wiping their boots when they drops by. I'll get me a straight-laced, uncomplicated, almost fulfilling sex life by picking out the right movies and changing the sheets on a regular basis.

N – I dont even know how to cook. I have *never* watched the news and have no desire to. When is that supposed to kick in? I'm always at least a day behind on garbage day. I'm obviously not dumb, that's obvious. Obviously. So you think I could figure that out.

K – I'm gettin' a new toothbrush, maybe a fancy seven dollar electric one. "That wet towel doesnt belong on the bedroom floor!" "Oh I'm sorry, is it my turn to do the dishes?"

N – And I know he's an asshole, and a liar, and a thief, but he made me feel safe. When nothing and no one else did. Safe safe safe safe. Keith Kavanagh is crazy. So nothing could touch me. I'm not so crazy, you know? He knew how to make me feel totally totally safe.

K – I'll be walking a four legged dog and curling up to the Wednesday night sitcom marathon. I'll be constantly quitting smoking. And if you happens to open my fridge, you'll find light mayonnaise, whole grain bread, some kinda smoked fuckin' cheese, and some of that French fizzy water in the green bottle. We'll have *brunch*. Sure you'll have to compliment the curtains that match the carpet that goes right nice with the little place mats. I'll be sobering myself up too. "Can I offer you a cup of coffee? I'm sorry b'y, all's I got is decaf." Look here, I'll take my chances with the devil I dont know.

Keith huddles up on the step, using his bag for a pillow.

Cant be much worse than the one that I knows.

N – Even if he hides it most of the time, he's a smart duck. He's smarter than anyone else I know. And underneath that grease and behind that smoky stench, he's a real hunk. And he was mine. And I want him back. Oh Keith, if you were here now I'd screw you right here on this bench.

She flops down on the bench, passes out.
Keith slumps down on Natasha's step.

K – "Oh the girls got a cushion and the boys got a pin. The girls lies down and the boys...sticks it in."

Lights out.

Scene 4

K – She's standing over me. Her hair is brushing my face and it's the nicest thing I've smelled in a long time. The Natasha I fell in love with. With her long, careless blonde hair and the army boots, not the Natasha with the designer jeans and those fake leather platform fuckin' Aldo shoes. She's stroking my face, smiling and calling my name.

Natasha walks around the corner. She is immediately enraged, walks passed him, into the house and slams the door. Keith wakes with a start, looks around, disoriented then breaks into a verse from Bob Dylan's 'Shelter from the Storm'. Natasha comes back out, braced for a racket.)

N – What?

K – Hello little red riding hood.

N – You are stalking me, do you realize that?

K – Stalking?

N – And you're drunk.

K – How's it stalking? I came up for a visit. You dont want me here I'll go.

Keith walks offstage. Natasha calls his bluff for as long as she can. As soon as she stands up to see where he's gone Keith walks back to her.

K – ...Look, I just wants to talk...I came here because I loves you.

N – So what, I'm supposed to just fall into your arms? You're here to rescue me? I dont need rescuing. I'm happy for the first time in a long time.

K – Natasha. You're not happy up here...

N – You dont even know the meaning of the word. Happy people dont have to drink themselves into a stupor just to get to sleep every night.

K – C'mon 'Tash. Dont be pickin'...I dont want to do this out here on the street in front of everyone. Can we just go lie down?

N – You've been phoning me twenty-four seven for the past few weeks, leaving suicide notes on my message manager, and because I'm not a crisis hot-line and I dont respond right away, you automatically think I'm up here screwing around on you.

K – I didnt say a thing about you screwing around on me. I just wants to go inside. Come on, lets go in.

N – No, Keith, you are not coming in, you're a mess. You'll only break something.

K – Break something. What am I a big bull moose?

Natasha stares viciously.

K – Oh, I see what's going on…I'm interrupting.

N – Yes, you are, as a matter of fact. I got work to do.

K – Or maybe it's play?

N – Cheesy.

K – Move.

Keith tries to walk passed Natasha, they struggle. She gives him a good shove and he falls off the step. Keith lies still and silent.

N – Keith. Keith. You okay?

She goes to him to see if he's okay. After a moment, Keith jumps up, gives Natasha a shove and runs into the house.

N – You Asshole!

After a moment Keith comes out carrying some dried up flowers and a card, singing: Take me for what I am, A star newly emerging...

N – What?

He reads the card.

K – Thinking of you. You really are a star. Love Michel.
Natasha shouts over him.

N – He was my director, he directed me for my audition if your so smart.

K – Thinking of you. You really are a star. Love Michel.

N – What do you care, it's not like you didnt screw around on me for the past 3 years.

K – There she goes again with the screwing around. Got something to confess there superstar?

N – I was up in Toronto by myself in that shitty apartment bleeding and cramping while you were home screwing Monica, some slut who had the gall to leave her thongs in the couch.

K – Natasha...

N – Look, we cant work Keith, it will never work.

K – I never came up here to make it work. I came up here to make sure it was over. I needed to look into your eyes.

N – Well then get a good look Mr.-medicine-man. Windows to the soul.

K – What the hell is that supposed to mean now?

N – Oh because you think you're so deep and worldly. I spent the past year trying to communicate my emotions to you, trying to get you to treat me like I'm at least a step above the cat. But you're so wrapped up in your own image that you...

K – Natasha sweetheart I think we've heard all this. You needs some new material girl. Especially if you're going to make it as an actor. Or is that what's called your shtick?

Natasha screams in frustration.

N – An Actor? I want to be anything else but what I've become with you. You make me doubt myself and subsequently hate myself.

K – Sub-se-quent-ly. Subsequently. Nope, dont know that one.

N – Shut up! Shut up. Please. Shut up.

She grabs him by the face. He manages to grab both her wrists.

K – Have you been screwing around on me Natasha? Well...?

N – I wish I was.

K – Now is that what I asked?

She struggles free of his grip.

N – I've been hanging out with this guy who likes me and...

K – You think I couldnt get anyone if I went looking?

N – Oh I'm sure you have.

K – Well yes I can. I can indeed. I got a blow-job last night in the park.

N – Oh yeah off some hooker I'm sure.

K – If you're suggesting that I have to pay for it you're way off. No, it was just a girl who *liked* me. And it was good, for a change.

Long pause. Natasha is visibly hurt.

N – Is that true?

K – What if it is?

N – Then you're a drunken idiot.

K – And you're a fuckin psychopath, what else is new?

He goes to walk away. Natasha grabs him by the hair hauling him back.

N – Why do you call me that?

He shoves her off of him. She lunges after him, he grabs her hair and pulls her to the ground.

K – It's a good thing you did have an abortion, you're too psycho to raise a fuckin' youngster...

Natasha squeezes Keith's balls.

N – Yeah well it wasnt even yours.

Keith walks offstage.

N – You'd believe anything.

K – Not out of your mouth.

After a long pause Keith comes back.

N – Who gave you the blow job?

K – I made it up.

N – Yeah right.

Natasha goes for the house again. Keith breaks down.

K – WAIT! 'Tash no. Look I'm sorry. I'm sorry I wasnt there. I'm sorry...I'm sorry *I'm* not fit to have a child with. I'm sorry for all the hurt and...I left my fuckin' knapsack on the bus girl, come on...

N – You treat me like shit.

K – I didnt mean for any of this. I just lost sight of us, and how much you mean to me and...I dont want it to be over. I need you.

N – You dont give a fuck about me, or what I think.

K – I do.

N – Keith. Jesus Christ.

K – Please Natasha. I want us to find it again. No one knows me or sees me like you do. Please can we try again?

N – If I thought for a second that you'd sober up and straighten your shit out...

K – I can. I will.

N – I dont believe you.

K – Here, take it.

Keith hands her the rest of his booze. Natasha takes a swig. Keith lunges at her and kisses her until she pushes him away.

N – Your breath is rotten.

K – Yeah…well… yours is no prize.

Pause.

N – If you werent huddled on my step like a bum I'd be on the phone now booking a flight home. It's true. I'd decided.

Pause.

K – What about your big acting career?

N – Keith, see? How is that being supportive? I can find lots of work as an actor in St. John's. Acting is a state of mind.

K – Fuck does that mean?

N – I dont know.

They both have a little laugh. Awkward pause. They hug and kiss again.

N – Keith? What would you say if I told you I was never pregnant first nor last?

K – Come on, Natasha. Stop it. For fuck sakes cant you see that I'm fragile?

N – Go in, wash up and book yourself a ticket on the bus. You'd be lucky if you get home before me. I got some money.

Keith goes in the house. Natasha sits on the steps.

N – When will we know that enough is enough?

She puts her head in her hands then looks towards the audience.

Lights down.

Epilogue Scene

Lights up on Keith. He blocks his face with his forearms in case anyone finally decides to stone him to death. He creeps into the spotlight, grabs the bucket of rocks and places them a safe distance behind him.

KEITH – Too late. You had your chance.

He removes a pill bottle from his pocket and taps a couple into his hand. Swallows them dry. Throughout his monologue he scratches obsessively.

K – Bought these on the ferry off some greasy Caper Bretoner. As if there were any other kinds what? Anti-anxiety he said they were for. Anti-gravity is more like it. Oh, hey, I wrote something…

Keith, a little excited, pulls a piece of rumpled paper from his back pocket. He opens it up and prepares to read.

K – Ahem, "Requiem for the Devil You Dont Know"...

He stares at the page for a moment before crumpling it up in disgust.

K – Never even finished it...Least I havent drank yet. Well I had *a* beer. Just one. To keep the devils at bay...So I high-tailed it home like the proper fool. Did some tidying up. Bought some bread down to the gas station. And I would have bought the whole wheat shit too if they had it. I would. I mean I was really leaning that way. And...I...waited. And waited. Up pacing the floors. Imagine a grand and fantabulous fella like myself up pacing the floors over some young one. Lucky I didnt go out to the airport to meet her like I was thinking. So she gets a part in some silly little play. The Three Dollar Opera. Some German shit. Says it's going to take another month before she can come home out of it. I mean I dont resent her getting a bit of work but she's not even getting paid for fuck sakes. That's hardly what I calls a big break. And what am I supposed to do? I mean I cant...I dont...another month? Ahhh...sure I'm tough as nails though. Keith Kavanagh? I'm tough as nails. I can look after myself. She'll be back. See how you likes it. She'll be back. What? She'll be back.

Keith picks up the bucket and staggers off into the darkness.

The End

BIOGRAPHIES

JOEL THOMAS HYNES is the author of the internationally celebrated novels *Down to the Dirt* and *Right Away Monday*. He's also performed leading roles for numerous film, television and stage productions, including his own award-winning one-man show *Say Nothing Saw Wood* and the feature film adaptation of his novel *Down to the Dirt*.

Hynes teaches creative writing at Her Majesty's Penitentiary in St. John's, Newfoundland.

Winner of Newfoundland's prestigious "Artist of the Year Award" in 2009, SHERRY WHITE is an actor, screenwriter, producer, and director. She had a core role in the popular CBC TV series *Hatching, Matching and Dispatching* and was a writer and performer for that network's drama series *MVP*. White co-wrote the 2008 feature film adaptation of Joel Hynes' novel *Down to the Dirt* with Justin Simms. She also co-wrote and co-starred with Hynes in the play *The Devil You Don't Know*. White's directorial debut and award-winning feature film *Crackie* premiered at the Karlovy Vary International Film Festival in the Czech Republic in 2009 before its screening at the Toronto International Film Festival.

ACKNOWLEDGEMENTS

Resource Centre for the Arts
Amy House
Lois Brown
Ruth Lawrence
Sheila Sullivan
Percy Thomas
Jenny Rockett
Des Walsh
Red Watch Theatre Co.
Don Sedgwick
Shaun Bradley
Newfoundland and Labrador Arts Council.